High-Interest/Low-Readability Nonfiction

Extreme Places

by Kathryn Wheeler

Carson-Dellosa Publishing Company, Inc.
Greensboro, North Carolina

Credits

Editors:
Ashley Anderson and Carrie Fox

Layout Design:
Van Harris

Inside Illustrations:
Nick Greenwood

Cover Design and Illustration:
Nick Greenwood

A Sea without Fish

A big body of water in the middle of a desert sounds great, but the **Dead Sea** does not hold water that people or animals can drink. This big body of water between the countries of Jordan and Israel is the saltiest place on Earth. It is not really a sea at all; it is a lake. But, it is called a sea because it does not have freshwater.

Why is the Dead Sea so salty? It sits almost one-quarter of a mile below sea level. More than three million years ago, salt water from the Mediterranean Sea poured into a deep opening to form the Dead Sea. Today, water flows into the Dead Sea from the Jordan River and several streams. But, the water has no outlet, or way to leave after it flows in. Some of the water evaporates in the hot sun. Salt and other minerals are left behind.

Scientists say that the Dead Sea is actually sinking. It sits on a *rift valley*, an area where Earth's plates are spreading apart. During some years, the Dead Sea has sunk as much as 13 inches. And, people are using more water from the Jordan River, so less freshwater enters the Dead Sea every year. As it sinks lower and receives less freshwater, evaporation causes it to become saltier and saltier.

Lakes are usually filled with life. But, the Dead Sea lives up to its name. Nothing can stay alive there. There is no seaweed. No birds or animals can drink its salty water. If fish from the Jordan River swim into the Dead Sea by mistake, they die quickly. The water kills almost everything. It is at least seven times saltier than ocean water.

People like to visit this strange, quiet lake. The weather is hot and sunny. There are hotels and beaches. They float on the surface of the Dead Sea. People who have been swimming in an ocean and a pool will notice that it is easier to float in an ocean. That is because of the salt in ocean water. Because the Dead Sea has so much salt, it is hard to swim in it. But, the salt holds people's bodies up as if they were lying on rafts! It is actually harder to stand in the Dead Sea than it is to float. Some tourists even like to read books as they float on top of the water. When they come out, they are covered with salt.

Conversions
0.25 mile = 0.4 kilometer
13 inches = 33.02 centimeters

© Carson-Dellosa

Next Page

CD-104183 ® Extreme Places **15**

ISBN 978-1-60022-528-4

Table of Contents

Introduction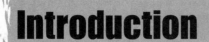

Struggling readers in the upper-elementary and middle grades face a difficult challenge. While many of their peers are reading fluently, they are still working to acquire vocabulary and comprehension skills. They face a labyrinth of standardized tests, which can be a nightmare for struggling readers. And, they face another major difficulty—the challenge of remaining engaged and interested while working to improve reading skills.

High-Interest/Low-Readability Nonfiction: Extreme Places can help! All of the articles in this book are written at a fourth-grade reading level with an interest level from grade 4 to adult.

Throughout the book, the stories use repeated vocabulary to help students acquire and practice new words. The stories are crafted to grab students' attention while honing specific reading skills, such as uncovering author's purpose; defining vocabulary; making predictions; and identifying details, synonyms, antonyms, and figures of speech. Most of the comprehension questions parallel standardized-test formats so that students can become familiar with the structure without the pressure of a testing situation. And, the articles even utilize the familiar "Next Page" arrows and "Stop" signs seen in most standardized tests. The questions also include short-answer formats for writing practice.

Best of all, this book will build confidence in students as they learn that reading is fun, enjoyable, and fascinating!

Note: Stories that include measurements, such as a length or temperature, also feature a convenient conversion box with measurements rounded to the nearest hundredth. Students will find this useful as they become familiar with converting standard and metric measurements. If students are not currently studying measurement conversion, simply instruct them to ignore the box. Or, cover it when making copies of a story.

So Much Water

Every September, the people who live in the town of **Cherrapunji, India**, start to worry about the coming dry season. It is strange that they are worried about having enough water. This place is one of the wettest places on Earth!

For four months every year, Cherrapunji is drenched with rain—450 inches of it! The rain comes down so hard that it rots crops in the ground. It washes away trees from the forest. During this *monsoon*, or downpour of rain and wind, it is hard for farmers to work. But then, the rain stops.

For the other eight months of the year, the people of Cherrapunji have a completely different problem. They do not have enough water. The forest that once surrounded the town helped trap rainwater and store it for the dry months. But now, many of the trees have been chopped down or washed away. The rainwater goes straight into the ground. And, the town is poor. The people cannot pay to build a system to store the water. So, people have to walk all day to get clean water. Every day, they collect buckets of water from springs outside the town.

Scientists are working on solutions. They say that people could put barrels outside to save rainwater as it falls from the roofs of houses. Scientists also think that replanting the forest will help keep the water from disappearing when it is needed most. Meanwhile, the people of Cherrapunji have to hike a long way to get water during the fall and winter. Sometimes, they are forced to buy water, even though they live in one of the wettest places on the planet!

Conversion

450 inches = 1,143 centimeters

Next Page

Name _____ Date _____

So Much Water

Answer the questions below.

1. The story describes all of the following problems EXCEPT—
   a. too much water for four months of the year.
   b. not enough water in the fall and winter.
   c. flooding of streets and houses.
   d. crops rotting in the ground.

2. Read the following sentence from the story and answer the question.

   Every September, the people who live in the town of Cherrapunji, India, start to worry about the coming dry season.

   Which of the following would be the result of a *dry season*?
   a. Trees wash away in the rain.
   b. Crops die because of the dry ground.
   c. There is not enough sun to grow crops.
   d. There is too much rain to plant food.

3. How do the people of Cherrapunji get water in the fall and winter?
   a. They collect rainwater.
   b. They hike to places that have water.
   c. They buy water.
   d. b. and c.

4. Cherrapunji gets about _____ inches of _____ during the spring and _____ .

5. Read the following sentence from the story and answer the question.

   Every day, they collect buckets of water from springs outside the town.

   Which word or phrase could be used to replace *springs* in this sentence?
   a. March, April, and May
   b. leaps
   c. water sources
   d. metal coils

6. Circle two adjectives that describe a monsoon.

   wet   windy   cold

   dry   sunny   hot

7. What is one way that the people of Cherrapunji might be able to save water?

   They can _____ the forests.

As Dry as a Bone

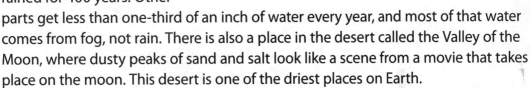

If you like dry places, you should go to the **Atacama Desert** in Chile. There are some parts of the desert where it has not rained for 400 years! Other parts get less than one-third of an inch of water every year, and most of that water comes from fog, not rain. There is also a place in the desert called the Valley of the Moon, where dusty peaks of sand and salt look like a scene from a movie that takes place on the moon. This desert is one of the driest places on Earth.

Why is the Atacama Desert so dry? It is actually found between two of the wettest places on Earth: the Pacific Ocean and the Amazon River. But, the Andes Mountains are in the way. They trap any rain that falls and hold it over the Amazon Rain Forest. The desert, on the other side of the mountains, gets none. Another interesting fact about the Atacama is that it is a cold desert. The average *elevation*, or height above sea level, is close to 8,000 feet. The temperature ranges from 32°F–77°F.

Do not think that there is no life in this desert. As in all harsh places on Earth, some plants and animals have found ways to survive there. A few small plants grow in this dry place. They have very long roots that reach the water deep in the ground. These plants feed insects and a few animals, such as foxes and llamas.

There are a few salt lakes in the desert that were made with water from the last ice age. Big flocks of flamingos fly to the salty lakes. They do not drink the water. Instead, they eat a type of red algae that grows there. Their diet is what makes them bright pink. The flamingos also build nests and raise their young on the salt lakes.

One other animal has found a way to live in the Atacama: human beings. They live in tiny villages scattered in the desert. They also live in large towns along the coast of the Pacific Ocean. Most of these towns serve as shipping ports. Many tourists arrive in these towns and take day trips into the huge, dry desert all around them.

Conversions

0.33 inch = 0.85 centimeter
8,000 feet = 2,438.4 meters
32°F = 0°C
77°F = 25°C

Next Page

As Dry as a Bone

Answer the questions below.

1. Which of the following is the BEST description of the Atacama Desert?
   a. It is a very large desert with mountains on one side.
   b. It is one of the driest places on Earth.
   c. It is one of the driest places on Earth, and it is a desert in Chile near the Andes Mountains.
   d. It is very dry, but some animals still live there, including human beings.

2. Read the following sentence from the story and answer the question.

   As in all harsh places on Earth, some plants and animals have found ways to survive there.

   What is a synonym for *harsh*?
   a. healthy
   b. safe
   c. useless
   d. severe

3. The _____ Mountains

   trap rain.

4. They hold the rain over the Amazon

   _____ .

5. The Atacama Desert receives

   _____ rain as a result.

6. Which of the following is an opinion?
   a. Flamingos eat algae from the salt lakes in the Atacama Desert.
   b. The Atacama Desert must be the hardest place on Earth to live.
   c. The Atacama Desert has some villages and towns.
   d. Some animals cannot live in the Atacama Desert.

7. Read the following sentence from the story and answer the question.

   There is also a place in the desert called the Valley of the Moon, where dusty peaks of sand and salt look like a scene from a movie that takes place on the moon.

   Which of the following is the definition of *peaks* as it is used in the sentence?
   a. the height of achievement
   b. mountains
   c. quick looks
   d. curious glances

8. Would you like to go to the Atacama Desert? Why or why not? Write your answer in a complete sentence.

   _____

   _____

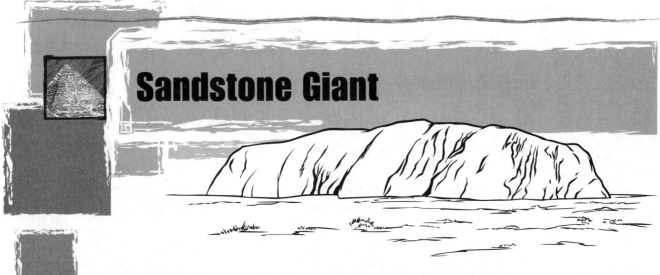

Sandstone Giant

People often stand looking at the huge sandstone rock. It rises more than 1,000 feet from the floor of the desert. If someone decides to walk all of the way around the huge rock, he will walk almost six miles! When the sun sets on the rock, the red sandstone seems to change colors. The rock turns purple and blue. This magical place is **Uluru**, and it is found in the middle of Australia.

Uluru is the native name of the giant rock. It is also known as **Ayers Rock**. Many ancient drawings are found on the rock and in its caves. Native Australians tell stories and legends about this strange place and how the rock came to be. One story says that serpent creatures had great battles around the rock. Their weapons made the scars that are now the folds, grooves, and caves in Uluru.

Scientists think that Uluru was under the sea 500 million years ago. Now, it sits in the middle of the *outback*. That is the dry desert in the center of Australia. The rocky sides of Uluru have many caves. Small trees and grass grow in some places on the rock. Many birds and animals live there. There are also lizards, hopping mice, and kangaroos. Parrots and falcons also live on the giant sandstone rock.

The mound looks almost like it was made by humans, with long *ripples*, or folds, across its sides. During the day, the rock seems to change colors. This is because of the way light hits its folds and caves. It does not rain very much in the outback. But, when it does rain on Uluru, hundreds of waterfalls pour down the flowing sides of the mysterious sandstone giant.

Conversions
1,000 feet = 304.8 meters
6 miles = 9.66 kilometers

Next Page

Sandstone Giant

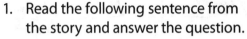

Answer the questions below.

1. Read the following sentence from the story and answer the question.

   Native Australians tell stories and legends about this strange place and how the rock came to be.

   What is an antonym for *strange*?
   a. mysterious
   b. awful
   c. weird
   d. everyday

2. Who named the rock *Uluru*? Write your answer in a complete sentence.

   _____

   _____

   _____

3. Which of the following is NOT a feature of Uluru?
   a. It changes colors at sunset.
   b. It has caves with ancient drawings.
   c. It has a lake on top.
   d. It is made of sandstone.

4.–8. Write T for true or F for false.

4. _____ One type of animal that lives on the rock is the lizard.

5. _____ Uluru is made of granite.

6. _____ Uluru's cave drawings were made by aliens.

7. _____ The land around Uluru is very wet and gets a lot of rain.

8. _____ There is a story that says that the caves on Uluru were made by serpent creatures.

9. Choose the word that BEST completes the following sentence:

   The dry, central part of Australia is called the _____ .
   a. backout
   b. outboard
   c. outland
   d. outback

10. Circle three synonyms for the word *huge*.

gigantic	rippled	dry
magical	sandstone	giant
colorful	mysterious	large

STOP

Extreme Erosion

The **Grand Canyon** is one of the natural wonders of the world. The gigantic canyon is in the southwestern United States. It was carved out of the rock by the Colorado River. It took more than six million years for the river to make the huge canyon. The Grand Canyon is 277 miles long, and it is almost 1 mile deep in most places.

Today, the Colorado River snakes through the bottom of the Grand Canyon. Visitors can stand on one of the *rims*, or top edges, of the canyon. When they look across, they see huge striped rocks, hills, valleys, and towering canyon walls. The whole canyon covers more than one million acres of land. That is bigger than the state of Rhode Island!

The walls of the canyon are striped because they show layers of rock. The oldest rocks are at the bottom of the canyon. They are almost 2 billion years old. The youngest rocks are at the top of the canyon. They are 270 million years old. *Geologists*, or scientists who study the formation of Earth, have studied these layers for years. Each layer represents a part of time in Earth's history. The Grand Canyon is the only place on the planet where so many different layers can be studied so easily.

The canyon is also home to more than 2,000 plant and animal species. Many of them are very rare, and some are found only at the Grand Canyon. Many of the species are endangered or protected.

Because the Grand Canyon is so large and deep, it has five different *life zones*. That means that the canyon has five areas with completely different animals and plants. Each life zone is found at a different *elevation*, or height above sea level. So, each zone has a different *climate*, or type of weather. And, each zone has a different amount of water. All of these things affect the types of plants and animals that can live in each zone of this rare and extreme place.

Conversions

277 miles = 445.79 kilometers
1 mile = 1.61 kilometers
1,000,000 acres = 404,685.64 hectares

Next Page

Name_____ Date_____

Extreme Erosion

Answer the questions below.

1. Which of the following is NOT a feature of the Grand Canyon?
   a. valleys
   b. striped rock walls
   c. hills
   d. sand dunes

2. What is a *geologist*?
   a. a scientist who studies dinosaurs
   b. a scientist who studies the formation of stars
   c. a scientist who studies the formation of Earth
   d. a scientist who studies plants and animals

3. Read the following sentence from the story and answer the question.

   Today, the Colorado River snakes through the bottom of the Grand Canyon.

   What is the definition of *snakes* as it is used in this sentence?
   a. winds
   b. sneaks
   c. more than one snake
   d. mean people

4. The Grand Canyon is so huge that it

   has _____ different life zones.

5. The _____

   River carved the Grand Canyon.

6. It took more than _____

   years to form the Grand Canyon.

7. The canyon is almost _____

   _____ deep in most places.

8. Which of the following is an opinion?
   a. The Grand Canyon is the most beautiful place in the United States.
   b. The Grand Canyon is almost one mile deep.
   c. The Grand Canyon is filled with hills, valleys, and high cliff walls.
   d. Many rare plants and animals live in the Grand Canyon.

9. Why are there so many different life zones in the Grand Canyon? Write your answer in complete sentences.

   _____

   _____

   _____

   _____

   _____

An Underwater Wilderness

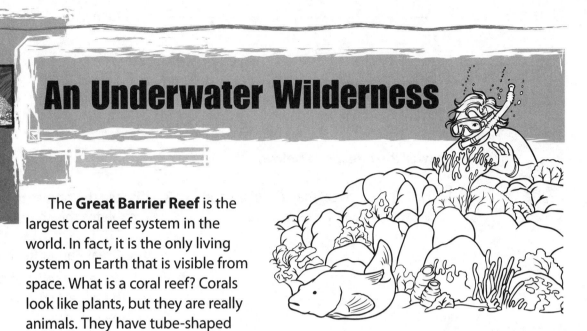

The **Great Barrier Reef** is the largest coral reef system in the world. In fact, it is the only living system on Earth that is visible from space. What is a coral reef? Corals look like plants, but they are really animals. They have tube-shaped bodies with mouths on top. When corals die, their hard outer skeletons stay in the water. Then, sand and small stones get washed between the skeletons. New coral grows on top of the old coral skeletons. The reef is built this way, layer by layer.

The Great Barrier Reef is not just one reef. It is actually thousands of smaller reefs all forming parts of a huge system. It is also made of hundreds of coral islands. The huge reef system stretches along the coast of Australia. It is more than 1,200 miles long and covers more than 135,000 square miles. That is an area bigger than the country of Poland!

Between the reef and the beach is a *lagoon*, a protected area of shallow water. It is a great place for sea life because it is warm and quiet. Divers love to dive there. There are more than 1,500 different kinds of fish living in this underwater wilderness. And, more new species are discovered every year.

Divers also find many sizes of fish under the waves around the reef. There are red dwarf gobies. These tiny fish are less than one-half of an inch long. One type of shark that visits the reef is the whale shark. It is the largest known living fish species, and it can grow to be more than 40 feet long!

The reef is a great place for divers to explore because of the bright, colorful fish and many other kinds of sea life. Divers might also see one of the many shipwrecks. This part of the ocean is a hard place to sail because of its reefs, islands, and shallow water. Today, there are many lighthouses along the beaches. They help ships steer clear of the dangers at the Great Barrier Reef.

Conversions

1,200 miles = 1,931.21 kilometers
135,000 miles^2 = 349,648.39 kilometers^2
0.5 inch = 1.27 centimeters
40 feet = 12.19 meters

Next Page

Name _____ Date _____

An Underwater Wilderness

Answer the questions below.

1. How is a *coral reef* made? Write your answer in complete sentences.

   _____

   _____

   _____

   _____

   _____

2. The Great Barrier Reef has all of the following features EXCEPT—

   a. coral islands.
   b. many kinds of sea animals.
   c. a giant underwater canyon.
   d. a lagoon.

3.–7. Write T for true or F for false.

3. _____ The Great Barrier Reef is more than 10,000 miles long.

4. _____ One type of animal found at the reef is a red dwarf goblin.

5. _____ The Great Barrier Reef is not one reef, but many.

6. _____ Giant sharks can be found at the reef.

7. _____ Lighthouses help keep ships away from the reef.

8. Choose the phrase that BEST completes this sentence:

   The Great Barrier Reef is _____.

   a. along the coast of Australia.
   b. the largest coral reef system in the world.
   c. an underwater mountain range.
   d. a. and b.

9. In the lagoon, explorers have found—

   a. more than 300 shipwrecks.
   b. more than 1,500 types of fish.
   c. more than 50,000 lighthouses.
   d. none of the above.

10. The Great Barrier Reef's lagoon is a good place for divers because—

   a. there are no clams.
   b. the water has a lot of waves.
   c. there are so many kinds of unusual sea life.
   d. b. and c.

A Sea without Fish

A big body of water in the middle of a desert sounds great, but the **Dead Sea** does not hold water that people or animals can drink. This big body of water between the countries of Jordan and Israel is the saltiest place on Earth. It is not really a sea at all; it is a lake. But, it is called a sea because it does not have freshwater.

Why is the Dead Sea so salty? It sits almost one-quarter of a mile below sea level. More than three million years ago, salt water from the Mediterranean Sea poured into a deep opening to form the Dead Sea. Today, water flows into the Dead Sea from the Jordan River and several streams. But, the water has no *outlet*, or way to leave after it flows in. Some of the water evaporates in the hot sun. Salt and other minerals are left behind.

Scientists say that the Dead Sea is actually sinking. It sits on a *rift valley*, an area where Earth's plates are spreading apart. During some years, the Dead Sea has sunk as much as 13 inches. And, people are using more water from the Jordan River, so less freshwater enters the Dead Sea every year. As it sinks lower and receives less freshwater, evaporation causes it to become saltier and saltier.

Lakes are usually filled with life. But, the Dead Sea lives up to its name. Nothing can stay alive there. There is no seaweed. No birds or animals can drink its salty water. If fish from the Jordan River swim into the Dead Sea by mistake, they die quickly. The water kills almost everything. It is at least seven times saltier than ocean water.

People like to visit this strange, quiet lake. The weather is hot and sunny. There are hotels and beaches. They float on the surface of the Dead Sea. People who have been swimming in an ocean and a pool will notice that it is easier to float in an ocean. That is because of the salt in ocean water. Because the Dead Sea has so much salt, it is hard to swim in it. The salt holds people's bodies up as if they were lying on rafts! It is actually harder to stand in the Dead Sea than it is to float. Some tourists even like to read books as they float on top of the water. When they come out, they are covered with salt.

Conversions

0.25 mile = 0.4 kilometer
13 inches = 33.02 centimeters

Next Page

A Sea without Fish

Answer the questions below.

1. Read the following sentence from the story and answer the question.

   But, the Dead Sea lives up to its name.

   Why does the author say this?
   a. Nothing can live in the Dead Sea.
   b. The Dead Sea is really a lake.
   c. People cannot go into the water of the Dead Sea.
   d. The Dead Sea is too quiet.

2. The Dead Sea is found—
   a. between Jordan and Egypt.
   b. between Israel and Iraq.
   c. between Israel and Lebanon.
   d. none of the above

3. Which of the following is NOT a fact?
   a. The Dead Sea is below sea level.
   b. I would not like to try to swim in the Dead Sea.
   c. The water of the Dead Sea is at least seven times saltier than ocean water.
   d. The Dead Sea is found in the middle of a desert.

4. Which of the following is NOT explained in the story?
   a. how the Dead Sea became so salty
   b. how the Dead Sea is sinking even lower
   c. what happens to fish that swim into the Dead Sea
   d. how people use minerals from the Dead Sea in spa treatments

5. Which of the following defines *outlet* as it is used in the story?
   a. a place to buy clothing
   b. a place to plug in a lamp
   c. a place for water to go after it has flowed into a lake
   d. a way to show feelings

6. Would you like to swim in the Dead Sea? Why or why not? Write your answer in complete sentences.

   _____

   _____

   _____

   _____

   _____

   _____

STOP

Legendary Lake

The biggest body of freshwater in the world is a place of many legends. Much of its shoreline is covered with forests and rocky cliffs. There are also ports, and many large ships travel on this great lake. This lake is **Lake Superior**, the northernmost of the Great Lakes. It is located in North America, along the border of the United States and Canada.

How big is Lake Superior? Its surface covers about 31,700 square miles. That is almost as large as the country of Austria. In addition to being large, Lake Superior is also a cold, deep lake. At its deepest point, it is more than 1,300 feet deep. Some of the world's tallest buildings could fit underwater at that depth!

In fact, Lake Superior is big enough to hold the water from all of the other Great Lakes. Then, it could still hold the water from three more lakes that are the size of Lake Erie. If someone poured out all of Lake Superior's water, it would cover the continents of North and South America in one foot of freshwater.

Storms form quickly on Lake Superior. Sometimes, the lake water is covered in fog, even when the weather on land is clear and sunny. In the fall, the lake can be very dangerous for ships. *Gales*, storms with strong winds, can start without warning. Gale winds have caused waves that were more than 30 feet high. The lake's stormy nature causes problems for some of the boats and ships that try to cross it.

Lake Superior is the resting place for the wrecks of more than 350 ships. Most sank during big fall storms. Many of the wrecks are found by divers along the rocky coast of the northern shore of Lake Superior. And, because the lake is very clear, it is a popular site for divers. There have been shipwrecks on the lake since fur traders started crossing it in canoes in the 1700s. Many legends are told about the shipwrecks, the dangers, and the history of this vast northern lake.

Conversions
31,700 miles^2 = 82,102.62 kilometers^2
1,300 feet = 396.24 meters
1 foot = 30.48 centimeters
30 feet = 9.14 meters

Next Page

Legendary Lake

Answer the questions below.

1. Read the following sentence from the story and answer the question.

   The lake's stormy nature causes problems for some of the boats and ships that try to cross it.

   What is the definition of *nature* as it is used in the sentence?

   a. plants
   b. animals
   c. temperament
   d. scenery

2. Which of the following sentences about the shipwrecks on Lake Superior is true?

   a. Fewer than 35 wrecks are found there.
   b. Most of the ships sank during spring storms.
   c. There have been shipwrecks on the lake since the 1700s.
   d. Many of the wrecks are found along the eastern shore of the lake.

3. The story describes all of the following EXCEPT—

   a. American Indian stories about Lake Superior.
   b. that Lake Superior is the largest body of freshwater in the world.
   c. that Lake Superior is dangerous for ships in the fall.
   d. shipwrecks in Lake Superior.

4. How big is Lake Superior?

   a. Its surface area is 31,700 square miles.
   b. It is deep enough to hold a skyscraper.
   c. It can hold all of the water from the other Great Lakes.
   d. all of the above

5. *Gale* means—

   a. a storm with a lot of rain.
   b. a storm with dangerous winds.
   c. a calm, clear day.
   d. a light rain.

6. *Legends* are—

   a. facts.
   b. songs.
   c. stories.
   d. disasters.

7. Which fact from the story seems most surprising to you? Why? Write your answer in complete sentences.

   _____

   _____

   _____

   _____

   _____

STOP

"Dino"-Mite!

When you think about dinosaurs, do you think about Canada? You should! One of the best places to find dinosaur bones is in the province of Alberta, Canada. It is the **Dinosaur Provincial Park**, and it is found in a large valley. The valley was made at the end of the last ice age. Water from the melting ice cut into the ground and made a rock-filled river. Today, the park is in Canada's *badlands*, an area with high cliffs, little water, and rocky ground. Badlands are created when a lot of wind and water cause deep erosion. Erosion uncovers things that have been buried for many years, like dinosaur bones and other fossils.

More than 75 million years ago, the badlands looked very different. The area was warm and had a lot of water. The ground was wet and swampy. It was a great place for dinosaurs to find food. Scientists know this because they have found so many dinosaur bones there. It is rare to find even one whole dinosaur skeleton. But here, scientists have found at least 150 whole dinosaur skeletons! They have also found big piles of dinosaur bones called *bone beds*.

There is one bone bed that has only Centrosaurus bones in it. These huge, elephant-like dinosaurs lived in herds. Scientists think that many members of a herd drowned when they tried to cross a flooded river. All of their bodies sank into the river bed. Today, scientists are still finding hundreds of bones there.

Tourists who go to the dinosaur park can visit a museum to see some of the skeletons. They can also see actual places where scientists have looked for bones. People can take tours to see the badlands and other digs that are still in progress.

Scientists have found the bones of at least 38 different types of dinosaurs in the park. Because the ground was once wet, the bones are in good shape. Leaves from different types of plants that once grew there have also been found. With all of these fossils in Canada's Dinosaur Provincial Park, we can learn what life was once like.

Next Page

"Dino"-Mite!

Answer the questions below.

1.–5. Match each word to its antonym.

1. _____ huge   a. smooth

2. _____ best   b. dry

3. _____ rocky   c. tiny

4. _____ wet   d. bad

5. _____ good   e. worst

6. The Centrosaurus was—
   a. a type of fossil.
   b. a big, elephant-like dinosaur.
   c. a snake-like dinosaur.
   d. a type of scientific process.

7. What types of fossils have been found at the dinosaur park?
   a. dinosaur bones and small fish
   b. rocks and trees
   c. dinosaur bones and plant leaves
   d. dinosaurs and snails

8. A bone bed is _____

   _____

   _____ .

9. The valley of the dinosaur park was

   made by _____

   _____

   _____ .

10. Scientists have found bones from at

    least _____ types of

    dinosaurs at the dinosaur park.

11. Why is it so exciting to have found 150 whole dinosaur skeletons in one place?
    a. Usually, people find many more skeletons.
    b. It is unusual to find even one whole dinosaur skeleton.
    c. It is easy to find skeletons, but not all in the same place.
    d. It is strange to find so few skeletons in the same place.

12. Would you like to help dig for dinosaur bones? Why or why not? Write your answer in complete sentences.

    _____

    _____

    _____

    _____

    _____

    _____

STOP

Terrific Tides

Can the moon touch Earth? In a way, it does. The pull of the moon's gravity on the planet is what causes *tides*. Water moves as the moon travels around Earth. In most places, high and low tides are just a part of everyday life. The water moves only a few feet, back and forth. But, in the **Bay of Fundy**, things are different.

This deep, narrow bay is in Nova Scotia, Canada. It is shaped like a funnel. The water in the bay moves back and forth constantly with the biggest tides in the world. The extreme tides that are created here make the Bay of Fundy known worldwide.

Wolfville is one town on the Bay of Fundy. When the tide is high, fishing boats float on the water. Just a few hours later, there is no water at all! The average difference between high tide and low tide is more than 45 feet of water. At low tide, boats sit on the mud. People can walk out onto the muddy floor of the bay. Thousands of birds come to eat the small fish and worms left behind by the tide.

When it is time for high tide, look out! More than 100 billion tons of water rush from the ocean into the bay in one big wave. The weight of all of that water actually bends the ground around the bay. In some places, it makes rivers and streams reverse directions. This is called a *tidal bore*. A tidal bore happens when the incoming tide pushes upstream against the usual flow of the water.

Cape Split is a rocky cliff that juts into the Bay of Fundy. At this place, you can hear a huge roaring sound. It is the sound of the rushing water forcing its way back into the bay. The people who live on the Bay of Fundy say that this noise is "the voice of the moon."

Conversions
45 feet = 13.72 meters
100 billion tons (U.S.) = 90,718,474 tons (metric)

Next Page

Terrific Tides

Answer the questions below.

1. _____ are made by the pull of the moon's gravity on Earth.

2. One town on the Bay of Fundy is

   _____ .

3. Normal tides change the water level only by _____ feet.

4. At the Bay of Fundy, the average difference between high and low tide is more than _____ feet.

5. Read the following sentence from the story and answer the question.

   In most places, high and low tides are just a part of everyday life.

   Which word could replace *everyday* in this sentence?

   a. weekly
   b. exciting
   c. engaging
   d. normal

6. The story mentions all of the following places EXCEPT—

   a. the Bay of Fundy.
   b. Wolf Cove.
   c. Cape Split.
   d. Canada.

7. The title of this story is "Terrific Tides." What is a synonym for *terrific* as it is used in the title?

   a. tremendous
   b. tiny
   c. terrible
   d. trickling

8. The author says that people at the Bay of Fundy call the roaring sound of the tide "the voice of the moon." Why do you think they say this? Write your answer in complete sentences.

   _____

   _____

   _____

   _____

   _____

   _____

STOP

Ocean Gateway

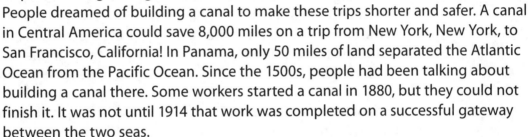

In the 1800s, ships had to make the long trip around the tip of South America to get from the Atlantic Ocean to the Pacific Ocean. The ships faced huge, dangerous storms. People dreamed of building a canal to make these trips shorter and safer. A canal in Central America could save 8,000 miles on a trip from New York, New York, to San Francisco, California! In Panama, only 50 miles of land separated the Atlantic Ocean from the Pacific Ocean. Since the 1500s, people had been talking about building a canal there. Some workers started a canal in 1880, but they could not finish it. It was not until 1914 that work was completed on a successful gateway between the two seas.

It took 10 years, thousands of workers, and millions of dollars to dig the **Panama Canal**. Building the canal was hard. The United States took over the work from France. Because of the mountains between the two oceans, the canal had to be built with *locks*. Locks are *chambers*, or sections, that fill with water or drain it away. The finished Panama Canal has 12 chambers in its series of locks. When the canal was built, it was the biggest set of locks and lock gates that had ever been created.

When a ship enters one side of the canal, big, thick gates close at each end of the chamber. Water pours through pipes and the locks raise the ship 85 feet above sea level. Then, the gates facing the front of the ship open. The ship can safely go through to the next chamber. Then, the ship crosses Gatun Lake to the other side of the canal. There, water is drained away in each chamber and another set of locks lowers the ship back to sea level.

Today, more than 40 ships go through the canal every day. It can take up to 10 hours for a ship to travel from one end of the canal to the other. The ships wait in line and take turns. Most of the ships carry cargo. They carry grain, iron ore, new cars, and other products. Some ships also carry passengers. More than one-quarter of a million passengers travel through the great canal every year.

Conversions

8,000 miles = 12,874.75 kilometers
50 miles = 80.47 kilometers
85 feet = 25.91 meters

Next Page

Ocean Gateway

Answer the questions below.

1. Which of the following is an opinion?

   a. In 1914, the Panama Canal was the largest system of locks ever created.
   b. People had been talking about building a canal since the 1500s.
   c. A canal was started in 1880.
   d. The Panama Canal is the greatest construction achievement in the world.

2. Which of the following is NOT described in the story?

   a. what happened to the workers who built the Panama Canal
   b. some types of cargo that are carried through the canal
   c. how the Panama Canal helped shorten the length of boat trips
   d. when the canal was finished

3. Read the following sentence from the story and answer the question.

   More than one-quarter of a million passengers travel through the great canal every year.

   Which phrase could the author have used in place of *one-quarter of a million passengers*?

   a. 25,000 passengers
   b. 200,000 passengers
   c. 250,000 passengers
   d. 2,500,000 passengers

4. Why was the Panama Canal built with locks?

   a. The locks are needed for faster travel.
   b. The locks raise and lower ships to the right level at each point along the canal.
   c. The locks help heavy ships pass through the canal.
   d. The locks are not necessary.

5. Which of the following sentences is NOT true?

   a. The Panama Canal was finished in 1904.
   b. The Panama Canal cut 8,000 miles off a sea trip from New York City to San Francisco.
   c. The Panama Canal contains 12 lock chambers.
   d. It can take 10 hours to get through the Panama Canal.

6. Why did builders decide that Panama was the right place to dig the canal? Write your answer in a complete sentence.

   _____

   _____

   _____

What a Wall!

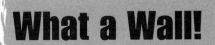

The most famous wall in the world is actually not just one wall. Are you surprised? Many people think that the **Great Wall of China** is one long wall. But, it is not. It is a series of walls and towers. There are open spaces between some of the sections. The wall is 3,000 miles long.

Why was this giant wall built? The first Great Wall of China was built in the 3rd century to protect the northern border of China against enemies. Later, in the 15th and 16th centuries, the wall we know today was built. It was made for the same reason—to protect China. The tribes that lived north of the wall were *nomads*, people who move from place to place. They raided China for food and cloth. The wall helped keep them out. Guards stood on the towers and watched the border.

The Great Wall of China is the longest man-made structure on Earth. Millions of workers labored on the wall in the 1400s and 1500s. The emperor said that it had to be wide enough for six soldiers on horses to ride side by side across its top. It took 200 years to finish all of the huge sections of the wall.

The Great Wall of China snakes across many hills. But, the wall is long and straight where it crosses plains and a desert. It ends when it reaches the Yellow Sea. The current wall was built using mostly earth, stones, and bricks. But, older sections of the wall are made of materials that were found nearby. In the mountains, many sections were built from stone. In the plains, builders used earth. And in the desert, they used sand.

Today, the Great Wall does not keep people out. In fact, it draws in many people. Some of the Great Wall has fallen or been destroyed over the years. Other parts are being fixed. Tourists from around the world visit the Great Wall, ruined or not. They can walk on its wide top. They can look across the hills and plains. It is like looking back in time.

Conversion
3,000 miles = 4,828.03 kilometers

Next Page →

What a Wall!

Answer the questions below.

1. Read the following sentence from the story and answer the question.

   The Great Wall of China snakes across many hills.

   Which word or phrase could replace *snakes*?

   a. crawls on its belly
   b. twists and turns
   c. hisses
   d. inches

2. The story describes all of the following details EXCEPT—

   a. the name of the emperor who started building the wall that we see today.
   b. the types of countryside that the Great Wall crosses.
   c. the enemies that the Great Wall kept out.
   d. how long it took to finish the sections of the wall.

3. Read the following sentence from the story and answer the question.

   It is like looking back in time.

   What kind of expression is this?

   a. a metaphor
   b. a simile
   c. an idiom
   d. onomatopoeia

4. What are *nomads*?

   a. people who do not have fixed homes
   b. people who move from place to place
   c. people who do not farm
   d. all of the above

5.–8. Write T for true or F for false.

5. _____ The emperor who started the first Great Wall lived during the 2nd century.

6. _____ The wall was built so that six guards on horses could ride side by side across it.

7. _____ There was another wall built before the one we know today.

8. _____ The Great Wall of China is one long, continuous wall.

9. What was the author's purpose in writing this story?

   a. to inform
   b. to persuade
   c. to entertain
   d. a. and b.

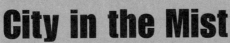

City in the Mist

The scene is amazing. High in the Andes Mountains of Peru is a city of stone. It looks like it is floating between two mountaintops. It is veiled by mist. This is **Machu Picchu**, a city built by the Incan people.

The city sits on a narrow ridge between two mountains. It is almost 2,000 feet above the river below. Machu Picchu was built in the 1400s. It was one of a series of villages and towns. This mountaintop city was probably a very important place for the Incas. Some people believe that it had vacation homes for important leaders and royalty. It was home to as many as 1,000 Incas.

Each house and temple in the city is built of stone. The stones were cut to fit together without using mortar. They fit together so perfectly that much of the city is still standing. Building the city was probably hard because the Incas did not have wheels during the 1400s. Scientists think that many strong men pushed the stones up steep ramps on wooden rollers.

Then, the Inca empire vanished. Spanish invaders stole gold from the Incas. They also spread *smallpox*, a dangerous disease that killed many Incas. Machu Picchu sat empty. It was forgotten by the outside world. But, in 1911, an American named Hiram Bingham rediscovered the city. He was guided by a 10-year-old boy. By then, the whole city was buried in vines and plants. It took years to clear away the vines and see the buildings underneath. Bingham found statues, temples, and one-room houses with inner courtyards. He also saw farms and places to store food. More than 100 staircases link the different levels of the city.

Bingham thought that after the Spanish took over the Incan towns near the rivers, the rest of the people fled to Machu Picchu for safety. There are no records that tell what happened to the people who once lived in this beautiful town high in the mist of the Andes Mountains.

Conversion

2,000 feet = 609.6 meters

Next Page →

City in the Mist

Answer the questions below.

1. Read the following sentence from the story and answer the question.

   There are no records that tell what happened to the people who once lived in this beautiful town high in the mist of the Andes Mountains.

   What does the word *records* mean as it is used in this sentence?
   a. flat discs that contain music or sound
   b. a way of capturing music so that it can be played back
   c. written accounts of something that has happened
   d. ruins of buildings

2. Which sentence BEST summarizes the main idea of the story?
   a. Machu Picchu was a place where the Incas had their temple.
   b. Machu Picchu was an important Incan city between two mountains, forgotten for years and then found again.
   c. Machu Picchu was where the Incas lived before they lost their riches to the Spanish and disappeared.
   d. Machu Picchu is a town made of stone.

3. What is *smallpox*?
   a. It is a type of Incan farm.
   b. It is a type of mountain city.
   c. It is a dangerous disease.
   d. It is a type of weather.

4. What is a *ridge*?
   a. a mountaintop
   b. a type of valley
   c. a valley below a mountain
   d. a piece of land that connects two mountains

5. The American who rediscovered Machu Picchu in 1911 was _____

   _____ .

6. Machu Picchu was built during the

   _____ .

7. Machu Picchu is found between

   two mountaintops in the

   _____ Mountains.

8. Machu Picchu is made of stones that

   were _____ so perfectly

   that the town still stands.

9. More than 100 _____

   connect the levels of the city.

STOP

Secrets of Giza

Most people know the **Giza Necropolis** by sight: three giant pyramids sitting on the desert sands of Egypt. Near them is a strange statue that has the body of a lion and the head of a human. The Giza Necropolis includes the **Great Pyramid**, two other large pyramids, and several smaller pyramids. The statue near it is the **Sphinx**. The Great Pyramid is one of the Seven Wonders of the Ancient World. It is the only ancient wonder left standing today. But, what do we really know about the pyramids?

The answer is, surprisingly little. Most scientists believe that the pyramids are about 2,000 to 5,000 years old, but they are not sure. How the pyramids were built is a mystery. The Great Pyramid alone is made of more than two million stone blocks. Some of the blocks weigh as much as 50 tons! How did people get these huge stone blocks into the desert to build the pyramids? The stones may have been brought up the Nile River on barges. Ramps were probably used to put each great stone in place. Scientists also make guesses about how long it took to build each of these huge structures. Some scientists think that each one could have taken as long as 40 years to build.

The pyramids are *tombs*, or places where great kings were buried. Each pyramid was shaped to look like a stone called a *benben*. The Egyptians thought that the benben stone had special powers because it pointed to the sun and the heavens.

The Sphinx is another mystery. Nobody knows who made this strange statue. No one is sure why it is near the tombs. Does it guard the tombs? Some scientists think that the Sphinx's face is really a *portrait*, or likeness, of a great king named Khafre. Khafre was buried in one of the three large pyramids at Giza. But, other people think that the Sphinx was built first, long before the pyramids and long before Khafre was buried. Today, scientists are working to uncover clues. Maybe someday they will know for certain when and how the pyramids and the Sphinx were built.

Conversion
50 tons (U.S.) = 45.36 tons (metric)

Next Page

Secrets of Giza

Answer the questions below.

1. What was the author's purpose in writing this story?
   a. to persuade
   b. to inform
   c. to inspire
   d. none of the above

2. Read the following sentence from the story and answer the question.

   Maybe someday they will know for certain when and how the pyramids and the Sphinx were built.

   Which word could replace *certain*?
   a. forever
   b. sure
   c. definitely
   d. detail

3. List three things that scientists do NOT know about the structures at Giza.

   a. _____

   _____

   b. _____

   _____

   c. _____

   _____

4. Which of the following is the BEST description of the structures at Giza?
   a. three pyramids and a statue of a lion
   b. four pyramids and a highway
   c. three large pyramids, a statue that has the body of a lion and the head of a human, and several smaller pyramids
   d. one giant pyramid and three small statues

5. What is a *portrait*?
   a. a special building in which a king is buried
   b. a style of building that points to the sun
   c. a likeness of someone's face
   d. a photograph

6. Would you like to visit Giza? Why or why not? Write your answer in complete sentences.

   _____

   _____

   _____

   _____

   _____

STOP

"Ice" to Meet You

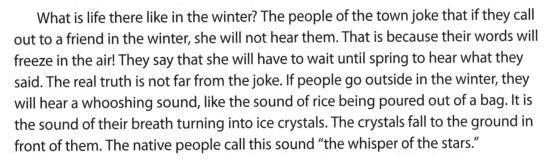

How would you like to have your milk delivered in big, frozen blocks? That is a part of life in **Verkhoyansk, Russia**, the coldest place in the northern hemisphere. The little town of 1,800 people is in Siberia. On its coldest winter day on record, the town endured a temperature of -90°F!

What is life there like in the winter? The people of the town joke that if they call out to a friend in the winter, she will not hear them. That is because their words will freeze in the air! They say that she will have to wait until spring to hear what they said. The real truth is not far from the joke. If people go outside in the winter, they will hear a whooshing sound, like the sound of rice being poured out of a bag. It is the sound of their breath turning into ice crystals. The crystals fall to the ground in front of them. The native people call this sound "the whisper of the stars."

The temperature makes life difficult. Sometimes, it is so cold that the trees explode and the foundations of houses split. That is because the wood contracts so much in the bitter cold. If people drink hot tea in Verkhoyansk, their teeth can crack. That is because of the extreme temperature change between the cold air and the hot tea. And, if people go outside and pour the tea out of their cups, it can freeze before it hits the ground.

Winter there is dark, as well as cold. On some days, the only daylight is a faint light, low in the sky. You may think that no one would want to live in such a cold, faraway place.

Conversion
-90°F = -67.78°C

Make a prediction.

What do you think the story will describe next?

_____

Next Page ➡

Answer the following questions based on what you read on page 31. Then, finish reading the story at the bottom of the page.

1. What is an antonym for *freeze*?
   a. harden
   b. crack
   c. muffle
   d. melt

2. Where is Verkhoyansk?
   a. Alaska
   b. Russia
   c. Siberia
   d. b. and c.

3. How cold can it get in Verkhoyansk? Write your answer in a complete sentence.

   _____

   _____

   _____

4. Circle three adjectives that describe winter life in Verkhoyansk.

   inviting   luxurious   difficult   tropical

   frigid   busy   dark   humid

In the past, there were some people who lived in Verkhoyansk unwillingly. When Russia was ruled by *tsars*, or emperors, the town was used as a prison. People were sent to live there as punishment.

But, other people are from tribes who have lived there for thousands of years. Outside the town, there are groups of nomads who live in the mountains. They are hunters. They also raise herds of reindeer. They say that it is actually warmer in the snowy mountains than it is in the town of Verkhoyansk! That is because the town is in a valley between the mountains. The coldest air comes into the valley, and the mountains hold it there. If there is no wind to move it, the air in the town is like the air inside a freezer—still, dry, and cold.

But, the people of the town have found ways to deal with the cold. They gather blocks of ice from the river and melt them on their stoves for water. And, they buy their milk in large, frozen disks. It is easy to carry "wheels" of milk home and melt them when they are ready to use them. That's life in Verkhoyansk!

"Ice" to Meet You

Answer the questions below.

5. Read the following sentence from the story and answer the question.

   If there is no wind to move it, the air in the town is like the air inside a freezer—still, dry, and cold.

   What kind of phrase is *like the air inside a freezer*?

   a. a metaphor
   b. a simile
   c. a synonym
   d. all of the above

6. What is the BEST description of why it is so cold in Verkhoyansk?

   a. It is so cold and dark in the wintertime because a person's breath freezes in the air.
   b. It is so cold because the town is in a valley and the mountains trap the cold air over the town.
   c. It is so cold because the wind blows so hard that it blows apart houses.
   d. It is so cold because Verkhoyansk is in Siberia and all of Siberia is just as cold as this town.

7. Which of the following is an opinion?

   a. Nobody would want to live in Verkhoyansk in the winter.
   b. In Verkhoyansk, milk is delivered in big, solid blocks.
   c. Outside Verkhoyansk, nomads raise reindeer and hunt.
   d. Verkhoyansk was once used as a prison area.

8. Which of the following is NOT true?

   a. If you drink something hot in Verkhoyansk during the winter, your teeth can crack.
   b. In Verkhoyansk, some house foundations crack in the winter.
   c. It is colder in the mountains outside Verkhoyansk than it is in the town.
   d. On Verkhoyansk's coldest day on record, it was -90°F.

9. What do the people of Verkhoyansk describe as "the whisper of the stars"?

   a. falling stars in the night sky
   b. the sound of a tree splitting in the cold
   c. the sound of a person's breath freezing and falling to the ground as ice crystals
   d. the sound of a herd of reindeer running down a mountain

10. Would you like to visit Verkhoyansk? Why or why not? Write your answer in complete sentences.

    _____

    _____

    _____

    _____

STOP

A Vast Desert

It is one of Earth's most difficult places to live—the great desert called the **Sahara**. This world of sand and rocks stretches across the top of Africa. It is about 1,000 miles from north to south and 3,200 miles from east to west. Almost one-fourth of the whole desert is made of sand dunes. Some of these dunes are huge. One dune in the country of Libya is as big as the entire country of France! The rest of the desert is made of flat, stony plains and jagged mountains.

The Sahara is one of the hottest places on Earth. It is also one of the driest. The whole desert gets fewer than three inches of rain each year. It can get as hot as 130°F. The lack of rain and the heat make this a very difficult place for life and travel.

But, people do live and travel in the Sahara. In fact, one of the most well-known trade routes in history crossed the huge desert. Nomads carried items like copper and salt across the sands. They used camels to carry these valuable goods to other countries. Nomads still live in the desert today. Many move from place to place looking for water for their families and their herds of sheep and goats. There are places across the desert that have small ponds and lakes. Date trees and palm trees grow there. Each of these places is called an *oasis*. People can get water and rest in the shade there. Animals stop there, too. Today, it can take days of traveling to find an oasis. But, at one time, there was much more water in the Sahara.

Conversions

1,000 miles = 1,609.34 kilometers
3,200 miles = 5,149.9 kilometers
3 inches = 7.62 centimeters
130°F = 54.44°C

Make a prediction.

What do you think the author will write about next?

_____

Next Page →

Answer the following questions based on what you read on page 34. Then, finish reading the story at the bottom of the page.

1. Read the following sentence from the story and answer the question.

   They used camels to carry these valuable goods to other countries.

   What is an antonym for *valuable*?
   a. meaningless
   b. worthless
   c. priceless
   d. useless

2. Where is the Sahara?
   a. Europe
   b. Asia
   c. Africa
   d. South America

3. How much of the Sahara is made of sand dunes?
   a. about one-half
   b. about one-third
   c. about one-fourth
   d. about one-fifth

   Thousands of years ago, the Sahara had more rain and more water. How do we know? Scientists have found clues. They have found shells and the bones of fish. They have found the remains of water animals, like hippos and crocodiles. It seems that many more animals lived in the desert at one time. Many more plants grew there, too.

   What happened to turn a lush, green place into today's desert? Scientists think that there was a big climate change. Strong winds blew the land dry. Today, it is still very windy in the desert. The winds are very important to the people who live in the Sahara. They can be very dangerous. Because of that, the people who live there have many words for the different kinds of wind. The *khamsin* is a wind that blows from March until May. This wind fills the air with sand. The fierce *harmattan* is a wind that blows so hard that it can take away a person's breath. Sometimes, it can create a heavy fog of sand that blocks the sun. This wind occurs during the winter months. A *sirocco* is a wind that blows very fast over a long distance, pushing dust and grit from Africa to Europe. All of these winds helped create the vast, dry Sahara.

Next Page →

A Vast Desert

Answer the questions below.

4.–7. Write T for true or F for false.

4. _____ A sirocco blows from March until May.

5. _____ Two trade route items of the Sahara were copper and sand.

6. _____ Scientists have found clues that show that the Sahara once had more water than it does today.

7. _____ The Sahara is one of the hottest places on Earth.

8. Which of the following statements is a fact?
   a. The Sahara must be the hardest place to live on Earth.
   b. It can get as hot as 130°F in the Sahara.
   c. The nomads probably have one place in the desert that they like best.
   d. It is likely that we will never know exactly how the climate changed in the Sahara.

9. What is an *oasis*?
   a. It is a place where date trees and palm trees grow.
   b. It is a place in the desert that has a small pond or lake.
   c. It is a place where people and animals stop to rest and have some water.
   d. all of the above

10. Read the following sentences from the story and answer the question.

    What happened to turn a lush, green place into today's desert? Scientists think that there was a big climate change.

    Which of the following is an example of a *climate change*?
    a. A place that was dry all summer has bad crops in the fall.
    b. A place that was warm in the winter suddenly gets snow every year.
    c. A place that floods in the spring has a flood in May.
    d. A place that is known for mud slides has its biggest mud slide ever.

11. The author mentions three different types of desert winds. Which one do you think would be the worst? Why do you think so? Write your answer in complete sentences.

    _____

    _____

    _____

    _____

STOP

Enormous Statues

At first, the Dutch sailors thought that the island was haunted. It looked so strange. Unlike most islands in the Pacific Ocean, this one was not covered with lush, green trees. It had bare hills. The few people who lived on the island did not have boats or canoes to take out to sea to fish, unlike most islanders in the Pacific. And, lining the hills were enormous, strange statues. They looked like men with huge heads and little bodies. Each statue that they saw was between 10 and 40 feet tall! The ship of Dutch explorers came to this strange place on Easter Sunday, 1722. That is why Europeans called it **Easter Island**.

Easter Island is lined with the huge statues. The statues are called *moai*. Each statue has an *ahu*, its own huge platform on which to stand. There are more than 880 statues on the island. Some stand in rows with their backs to the sea. Others are pushed over and broken. Still others are sitting in the quarry, where they were being carved. The tallest statue is found in the quarry. It is 72 feet tall.

Jacob Roggevenn, the explorer who found the island, saw the huge statues on this strange, stripped land. He wondered how the people who lived there could have made them. The island was created by three volcanoes, which meant there was a lot of soft, black rock to carve. But, the native people did not have trees that they could use to make wooden tools. They did not have plants that they could use to make ropes to help them stand up the statues or move them. They did not have boats that they could sail to other islands to trade for these things. The mystery of the huge statues and the strange, bare island took hundreds of years to solve.

Conversions

10 feet = 3.05 meters
40 feet = 12.19 meters
72 feet = 21.95 meters

? Make a prediction.

What do you think the author will write about next?

_____

Next Page

Answer the following questions based on what you read on page 37. Then, finish reading the story at the bottom of the page.

1. A man named _____

_____ was the

first European to see Easter Island.

2. The island has rows of giant stone

_____ .

3. Easter Island is in the _____

Ocean.

4. When the Dutch sailors saw Easter Island,

it had no _____ .

5. Easter Island was created by—
   a. coral.
   b. people.
   c. volcanoes.
   d. wood.

6. The island seemed strange to the Dutch sailors because—
   a. it had huge, scary caves.
   b. it had no people.
   c. it had a lot of trees.
   d. it was not like other Pacific islands.

Today, scientists think that Easter Island was destroyed because of the statues. People first came to the island between 400 A.D. and 700 A.D. It was a green, forest-covered place at that time. From clues on the island, scientists know that the native people made big boats from the trees. They caught large fish to eat. They made ropes from a tree called *hauhau*. They planted crops. But then, they started to make statues.

No one is sure why the statues were made. It might have been to honor dead ancestors. The native people carved more and more statues. They cut down trees and used the logs to roll the statues into place. Clans competed with each other to make the best statues. By about 1400, most of the trees on the island were gone. Animals could not live there any longer. The native islanders could no longer build boats and get food from the sea. Without trees, the good soil washed away, so they could not grow crops. The clans' extreme need to make the huge statues ruined their whole way of life. Today, only a handful of native people remain on Easter Island.

Easter Island

SOUTH AMERICA

Next Page

Enormous Statues

Answer the questions below.

7. Read the following sentence from the story and answer the question.

The clans' extreme need to make the huge statues ruined their whole way of life.

Which word could replace *ruined*?

a. chopped
b. stained
c. destroyed
d. preserved

8. Look at the chain of events below and answer the question.

People come to live on Easter Island between 400 A.D. and 700 A.D.

↓

Clans start to build huge stone statues.

↓

Topsoil washes away, and boats cannot be built.

↓

Jacob Roggevenn sees the island in 1722.

Which step is missing?

a. People on Easter Island chop down all of the trees to help move statues.
b. The statues are still standing on the island today.
c. Today, people on Easter Island still make ropes.
d. The Dutch build a town on Easter Island.

9. Which of the following sentences BEST summarizes the story?

a. Easter Island is known for its huge stone statues.
b. Easter Island is known for its huge stone statues, and these statues actually ruined life on the island.
c. Jacob Roggevenn was the first European to see Easter Island.
d. Today, Easter Island has no trees.

10. Which of the following is the name of the platforms on which the statues sit?

a. moai
b. hauhau
c. ahu
d. none of the above

11. Do you think that the loss of trees ruined life on Easter Island? Why or why not? Write your answer in complete sentences.

_____

_____

_____

_____

_____

STOP

City of Gold

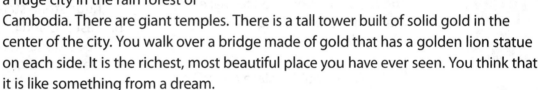

Imagine that it is the 13th century. You are walking through a huge city in the rain forest of Cambodia. There are giant temples. There is a tall tower built of solid gold in the center of the city. You walk over a bridge made of gold that has a golden lion statue on each side. It is the richest, most beautiful place you have ever seen. You think that it is like something from a dream.

A Chinese visitor named Zhou Daguan recorded these details after his visit to **Angkor**, an ancient city in the country of Cambodia. It was the great capital of an empire. It was the home of a people, called the Khmer, who controlled much of Southeast Asia and part of China. But, the empire fell to armies from Thailand. By 1432, the city was deserted. If it had not been for Daguan's writings, Angkor might have sounded like a fairy tale. The stories about it seemed to be just that—stories. But, the fact that the Chinese people also knew about the city made it seem more likely that Angkor was a real place.

While the rest of the world forgot about the once-beautiful capital, Angkor slept. Thieves stole the golden statues and tore down the golden tower. Vines and trees grew over the buildings and hid them. The temples in Angkor were built of stone. But, all of the other buildings were made of wood. These buildings rotted and fell apart as hundreds of years passed.

Monks rediscovered the temples when they were traveling through the rain forest. The monks created new stories, saying that ancient gods had built the temples. A few explorers might have seen the lost city of gold, too. But, it was not until the 1860s that the rest of the world heard about this hidden place.

Make a prediction.

What do you think the story will describe next?

_____

_____

Next Page

Answer the following questions based on what you read on page 40. Then, finish reading the story at the bottom of the page.

1. List three words or phrases that describe the ancient city of Angkor.

   a. _____

   b. _____

   c. _____

2. Who were the *Khmer*?

   a. temples
   b. explorers
   c. monsters
   d. rulers

3. Read the following sentence from the story and answer the question.

   You think that it is like something from a dream.

   What kind of phrase is *like something from a dream*?

   a. a metaphor
   b. a hyperbole
   c. an alliteration
   d. a simile

Henri Mouhot was a French explorer. He read a book about Siam, which is an old name for Thailand. It made him want to travel there. Mouhot spent more than three years in Southeast Asia. He traveled through the rain forest. He wrote a book in which he told about huge spiders that dropped onto his face as he tried to sleep. He found a guide who took him to the hidden city of Angkor. Mouhot wrote about the great temple, called Angkor Wat. It is the largest temple in the world. He told about stone carvings on the lower level of the great temple. He thought that they were the best he had ever seen. He described the other beautiful buildings that he found there. More than 70 temples were still standing.

Mouhot's writings outlived him. He died in 1861 and was buried along the Mekong River in the country of Laos. His book made people around the world want to see the great temple and the lost city. Today, thousands of people travel there every year. The temple of Angkor Wat is so important to the people of Cambodia that it is shown on their national flag.

Next Page ➡

City of Gold

Answer the questions below.

4. Henri Mouhot found more than

_____ temples, with stone

_____ that he thought

were the best he had ever seen.

5. Why were only the temples left standing in Angkor?
   a. An army destroyed the rest of them.
   b. The rain forest destroyed all of the other buildings in Angkor.
   c. The temples were built of stone, but the other buildings were made of wood, so they rotted.
   d. The other buildings were burned in a great fire.

6. Read the following sentence from the story and answer the question.

   Thieves stole the golden statues and tore down the golden tower.

   Which word could replace *thieves*?
   a. explorers
   b. raiders
   c. scholars
   d. adventurers

7. Which is a former name for Thailand?
   a. Angkor
   b. Wat
   c. Siam
   d. Mouhot

8. Why were the writings of Zhou Daguan so important?
   a. They showed that someone who was not Cambodian had been to Angkor.
   b. They showed that the stories about Angkor might not have been just legends.
   c. They told what the city once looked like before it was lost in the rain forest.
   d. all of the above

9. What would you look for if you could explore Angkor? Write your answer in complete sentences.

   _____

   _____

   _____

   _____

   _____

   _____

STOP

Inside the Rock

Nothing about the ancient city of **Petra** in the country of Jordan was ordinary. First, there was the way that people reached Petra. They did not walk on a path or an open road to reach this ancient city. Instead, they followed a winding canyon. Huge cliffs rose on both sides of the canyon. It was so narrow in some places that travelers were forced to walk or ride their animals single file. It was dark and cool. Then, suddenly, there was an opening, and they saw a huge, beautiful, red stone building called the Treasury. Today, the narrow canyon is still the main entrance to the ruins of Petra.

The canyon that leads to Petra is called the *Siq*. In ancient times, it had two important parts to play. First, the canyon made it easy to defend the city. No army could attack the city through such a narrow canyon. And second, the high walls of the Siq were filled with channels and pipes. They carried water into the desert town.

When it was first built, Petra was an Arab city. Later, it became a part of the Roman Empire. But during its entire history, it was a city for trading. It sat in the middle of an important trade route that crossed the desert. It was a place where travelers could find water and supplies.

During its 1,000-year history, people were building in Petra. Some of the buildings were not made of bricks or stone blocks. Instead, the buildings were carved into the sides of the huge, red sandstone rocks. That is why the city is named Petra, which means "the rock." Scientists are finding that Petra was not just a practical marketplace. It was an amazing and beautiful city.

Make a prediction.

What do you think the story will describe next?

Next Page

Name_____ Date_____

Answer the following questions based on what you read on page 43. Then, finish reading the story at the bottom of the page.

1. The first part of the story describes all of the following EXCEPT—
   a. how travelers reached Petra.
   b. how the buildings were made in Petra.
   c. what business was done in Petra.
   d. what scientists have found in Petra.

2. Which of the following is a synonym for *ancient*?
   a. up-to-date
   b. extraordinary
   c. old
   d. elaborate

3. Why was it easy to defend Petra?
   a. It had a very good army.
   b. It had many weapons that were used to keep away other armies.
   c. It was approachable only through a narrow canyon.
   d. It was a fort made of huge blocks of sandstone.

4. What is one adjective that describes Petra?

   _____

Scientists have been digging in the city of Petra for many years. They have explored the ruins. But, they have been able to look closely at only about one percent of "the rock." Petra was a very big city. Because it is so hard to reach, it was never changed or destroyed by invaders. The ruins still show the amazing carving skills of the people who lived there.

Explorers and scientists have found many beautiful carvings and statues. In a building called the Great Temple, there are carved pictures, carvings of elephant heads, and beautiful columns carved with leaves. Another temple holds statues of lions with wings. Many of the oldest statues are of figures from the zodiac. This was part of an early religion in Petra.

The people of Petra lived very well. Because of the trade route, the city was rich. Scientists have found coins and pieces of gold jewelry. They have found glass that was brought by Romans and bowls that were made by Arab tribes. Today, Petra is still filled with riches—the riches of its long and amazing history.

Name_____ Date_____

Inside the Rock

Answer the questions below.

5. Which of the following is an opinion?

   a. Petra sat on a trade route that went across the desert.
   b. Petra is probably the most beautiful ancient city that is still standing.
   c. The people who lived in Petra built many practical things.
   d. Petra became a part of the Roman Empire.

6. Read the following sentence from the story and answer the question.

   Nothing about the ancient city of Petra in the country of Jordan was ordinary.

   Which word could replace *ordinary*?

   a. commonplace
   b. exciting
   c. lasting
   d. sensational

7. What is the *Siq*?

   a. a city carved out of sandstone
   b. a narrow canyon that leads to the city of Petra
   c. a type of statue found in Petra
   d. none of the above

8. Which of the following is the BEST general description of Petra?

   a. It is a city in the desert.
   b. It is an ancient city of carved sandstone rock in Jordan.
   c. It is a city that had a system of pipes and dams for water.
   d. It is a huge city that scientists have not completely explored.

9. The author describes all of the following finds in Petra EXCEPT—

   a. temple statues of lions with wings.
   b. statues of figures from the zodiac.
   c. pieces of glass from Spain.
   d. columns carved with leaves.

10. What do you think is the most interesting thing about Petra? Why do you think so? Write your answer in complete sentences.

_____

_____

_____

_____

_____

_____

STOP

Time Stood Still

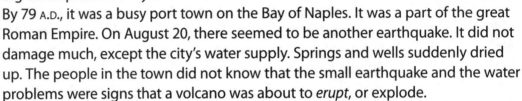

On the morning of August 24, 79 A.D., the people of **Pompeii, Italy**, woke for the last time in their beautiful town. Pompeii had already been rebuilt once after a big earthquake in the year 62 A.D. By 79 A.D., it was a busy port town on the Bay of Naples. It was a part of the great Roman Empire. On August 20, there seemed to be another earthquake. It did not damage much, except the city's water supply. Springs and wells suddenly dried up. The people in the town did not know that the small earthquake and the water problems were signs that a volcano was about to *erupt*, or explode.

Mount Vesuvius stood behind the town. It is a volcano. But, the people of Pompeii did not know that. After a normal morning on August 24, the volcano blew. A cloud of smoke and ash shot into the air. The blast was 12 miles high. It blocked the sun. Trees burned. Rocks rained on the town. Some people ran away. But, others stayed in their houses. They thought that it was safer to stay inside. They thought that the rocks and ash would eventually stop falling.

The rocks and ash did stop falling, but not until the town was almost buried. Then, something much worse happened. Fiery volcanic mud and red-hot magma shot out of the volcano. A blast of heat called a *surge cloud* rolled toward the town. When the blast hit Pompeii, the people who were still hiding in the town died. Time stopped in Pompeii. After a few weeks passed, the people who had fled the city tried to go back to see what had happened.

Conversion

12 miles = 19.31 kilometers

Make a prediction.

What do you think the author will write about next?

_____

Next Page

Answer the following questions based on what you read on page 46. Then, finish reading the story at the bottom of the page.

1.–5. Write T for true or F for false.

1. _____ Pompeii was destroyed by a flood.

2. _____ Pompeii was a town in Greece.

3. _____ Pompeii was built on the Bay of Naples.

4. _____ In the year 62 A.D., Pompeii was destroyed by an earthquake.

5. _____ Everyone in Pompeii knew that Mount Vesuvius was a volcano.

6. Which of the following words BEST completes this sentence?

   A volcano explodes, or _____ .

   a. exits
   b. interrupts
   c. erupts
   d. erodes

7. The first part of the story describes all of the following EXCEPT—

   a. what scientists have found in Pompeii.
   b. how people who were hiding in the town of Pompeii died.
   c. what Pompeii was like before the volcano exploded.
   d. where Pompeii was located.

Thousands of people were killed in Pompeii by the ash, the rain of rocks, and the blast of heat from the surge cloud. The people who escaped and returned weeks later found that the whole town was buried. They tried to dig tunnels into the town to find their houses and the bodies of those who had died. But, it was too hard. After a while, the people gave up.

Pompeii was a tomb. It remained buried for 1,700 years. It was not until the 1700s that people first started to dig up the buried town. The ash and mud had protected the city. Whole houses were still standing. The paintings on the walls were still clear. Scientists could even make casts of the bodies that they found. They were so detailed that they showed the expressions on the people's faces. Scientists have learned so much from this ancient place that was both destroyed and "saved" by a volcano.

Next Page

Time Stood Still

Answer the questions below.

8. Read the following sentence from the story and answer the question.

   Fiery volcanic mud and red-hot magma shot out of the volcano.

   What do you learn about *magma* from this sentence?

   a. Magma comes out of volcanoes.
   b. Magma is very hot.
   c. Magma can shoot out of a volcano.
   d. all of the above

9. What was the first thing that happened when Mount Vesuvius erupted?

   a. Rocks started raining on the town.
   b. A 12-mile cloud of smoke and ash blocked the sun.
   c. Magma and volcanic mud came out of the volcano.
   d. The people of Pompeii went out to sea on boats.

10. Why was so much of Pompeii so well preserved?

    a. It was frozen in ice for 1,700 years.
    b. It was buried in ash and rock by the volcano, so no one had touched it.
    c. It was dug up a few weeks after the volcano blast by the people who had escaped.
    d. It was flooded, and the whole city was safe underwater.

11. Most of the people who died in Pompeii were killed by a blast of heat called—

    a. a black cloud.
    b. a magma blast.
    c. a surgical cloud.
    d. none of the above

12. Scientists who dug up Pompeii made—

    a. new paintings for the houses.
    b. walls to keep out tourists.
    c. casts of the bodies of the people who died.
    d. a new core for Mount Vesuvius.

13. Why does the author say that Pompeii was *both destroyed and "saved" by a volcano*? Write your answer in complete sentences.

    _____

    _____

    _____

    _____

    _____

    _____

Top of the World

The people of Nepal call it "the forehead of the sky." The people of Tibet call it "the Goddess Mother of the World." In the west, people call it **Mount Everest**. It is the highest mountain on Earth, and it stands on the border of Nepal and Tibet.

Mount Everest towers more than 29,000 feet above sea level. It is an ever-changing place, filled with danger. The mountain is covered with large *glaciers*, or sheets of ice, that make it hard to climb. But, there are other dangers, too. The weather on Mount Everest can change quickly. From June through September, it is *monsoon* season. During this time, clouds cover the mountain. Snowstorms can start without warning. At other times, strong winds can whip across the face of the mountain. These winds can carry sand and stones that shower the ground and any people who are there.

The temperatures on Mount Everest are also extreme. It is never above freezing on the huge mountain. In the summer, the warmest day is still below freezing. In the winter, it can be as cold as -76°F!

Another danger on Mount Everest is *avalanches*, or huge pieces of ice and snow that break loose. They create big slides of snow that thunder down the mountain. An avalanche can change the whole shape of a mountain slope. Climbing routes can be covered. Valleys can be buried.

You might wonder why anyone would want to try to climb such a dangerous mountain. For more than 100 years, many people have tried.

Conversions
29,000 feet = 8,839.2 meters
-76°F = -60°C

Make a prediction.
What do you think the story will describe next?

_____

_____

Next Page →

Answer the following questions based on what you read on page 49. Then, finish reading the story at the bottom of the page.

1. A huge slide of snow on a mountain is called an _____ .

2. During monsoon season, _____ can cover Mount Everest.

3. _____ are sheets of ice that cover Mount Everest.

4. Mount Everest is the _____ mountain on Earth.

5. List two words or phrases that describe Mount Everest.

_____

_____

Native people did not try to climb Mount Everest before the early 1900s. They thought that it was the home of the gods. But, other people wanted to climb the huge mountain. There was a big problem, though. One side of Mount Everest is in Nepal. The other side is in Tibet. Nepal was closed to outsiders for many years. That left the Tibetan side of the mountain. It is the harder side to climb. In the 1920s, an explorer named George Mallory tried more than once to climb the north side of Mount Everest. He and another climber disappeared during his third attempt. In fact, many people have died on the mountain over the years.

Nepal opened its doors to outsiders in 1949. This meant that climbers could try to climb the south side of the mountain. That is still very hard to do, but it is much easier than climbing the north side. People from many different countries tried to be the first person to reach the top of Mount Everest. In 1953, two men finally made it. They were Edmund Hillary of New Zealand and Tenzing Norgay of Nepal.

Since that day, more than 3,000 climbers have beaten the odds. They, too, have made it to the *summit*, or very top, of Mount Everest. They have stood on the top of the world.

Top of the World

Answer the questions below.

6. Read the following sentences from the story and answer the question.

   In the 1920s, an explorer named George Mallory tried more than once to climb the north side of Mount Everest. He and another climber disappeared during his third attempt.

   Based on what you have read, what could have happened to Mallory?

   a. He could have lost his way during a snowstorm.
   b. He could have slipped and fallen on the icy face of the mountain.
   c. He could have been buried in an avalanche.
   d. all of the above

7. The story describes all of the following details EXCEPT—

   a. why natives did not try to climb Mount Everest before the 1900s.
   b. what kinds of food and supplies climbers need to pack.
   c. the names of the first two people who made it to the top of Mount Everest.
   d. the number of people who have climbed to the top since 1953.

8. One of the first people who climbed to the top of Mount Everest was—

   a. George Mallory.
   b. George Hillary.
   c. Tenzing Norgay.
   d. Benjamin Nepal.

9. Why do you think it took until the 1950s for someone to be able to climb to the top of Mount Everest?

   a. Until 1949, the easier way up the mountain was not open to outsiders.
   b. Until the 1950s, people did not have the right type of ropes to make the climb.
   c. Until 1953, climbers were not allowed into Tibet.
   d. none of the above

10. What does *summit* mean?

    a. the base of a mountain
    b. the face of a mountain
    c. the valleys of a mountain
    d. the very top of a mountain

11. Would you like to try to climb Mount Everest? Why or why not? Write your answer in complete sentences.

    _____

    _____

    _____

    _____

    _____

    _____

STOP

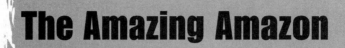

The Amazing Amazon

The **Amazon River** in South America is a mighty force. About 20 percent of the freshwater that goes into Earth's oceans comes from this extreme river. There is one river on Earth that is longer than the Amazon. It is the Nile River in Africa. But, the Amazon is wider and more powerful.

The Amazon is not easy to measure because it is a winding river. Its source is high in the Andes Mountains. Its water flows more than 4,000 miles to get to the sea. The *mouth* of the Amazon, or the place where the water reaches the sea, is more than 150 miles wide.

In fact, explorers discovered the mouth of the Amazon River in 1500. Their ship was 200 miles away from land on the Atlantic Ocean. But, the sailors found that they were sailing on freshwater! This was the flow of water coming from the huge mouth of the Amazon River.

The Amazon has not been changed much by people. In fact, the rain forest around the river has fewer people living there than almost any other place on Earth. It is true that people are cutting down rain forest trees at a fast rate. But, this is still an area without many buildings. In fact, the Amazon River does not have a single bridge built across it.

Maybe the lack of people is the reason why the Amazon River is the home to so many unique fish and animals.

Conversions

4,000 miles = 6,437.38 kilometers
150 miles = 241.4 kilometers
200 miles = 321.87 kilometers

Make a prediction.

What do you think the author will write about next?

_____

Answer the following questions based on what you read on page 52. Then, finish reading the story at the bottom of the page.

1. Read the following sentence from the story and answer the question.

   The Amazon River in South America is a mighty force.

   Which word could replace *force* in this sentence?

   a. pry
   b. strong
   c. power
   d. army

2. The Amazon River is—

   a. the second longest river on Earth.
   b. a supplier of one-twentieth of the world's freshwater.
   c. a river that starts in the Rocky Mountains.
   d. a river surrounded by plains.

3. The first part of the story describes all of the following about the Amazon River EXCEPT—

   a. where it is.
   b. how explorers first learned about it.
   c. what it looks like.
   d. what types of animals live there.

Many large fish and water mammals live in the Amazon River. A type of freshwater river dolphin, called a *Boto* or *Pink River Dolphin*, lives in this wide river. Catfish that live there can grow to weigh 200 pounds! Another type of fish that lives in the Amazon is the *piranha*, a meat-eating fish. These scary fish have sharp teeth.

There is even a type of snake that lives in the river. It is called the *anaconda*. It is one of the biggest snakes in the world. An anaconda floats just under the top of the water. Only its nose and eyes can be seen. Then, it waits for its next meal.

These animals share the river with thousands of rare animals from the rain forest. They all help make the Amazon River the amazing place that it is.

Conversion
200 pounds = 90.72 kilograms

The Amazing Amazon

Answer the questions below.

4. Which of the following is an opinion?

   a. The Amazon River flows 4,000 miles from the mountains to the sea.
   b. A type of freshwater dolphin lives in the Amazon River.
   c. The Amazon River must be the most extreme place on Earth.
   d. Fewer people live around the Amazon River than almost any other place on Earth.

5. What clue helped explorers know that a huge river was nearby?

   a. They were sailing on the sea, but the water under their ship was freshwater.
   b. They heard the roar of the river pouring into the sea.
   c. They saw types of fish that usually live in rivers.
   d. all of the above

6. Which of the following does NOT live in the Amazon River?

   a. catfish
   b. anaconda
   c. blue whale
   d. piranha

7. The story describes all of the following EXCEPT—

   a. what piranhas eat.
   b. why Botos are also called Pink River Dolphins.
   c. how anacondas hunt.
   d. how much the Amazon catfish can grow to weigh.

8. Would you want to go sailing on the Amazon River? Why or why not? Write your answer in complete sentences.

   _____

   _____

   _____

   _____

   _____

   _____

Extremely Active

Think about the first explorers who found the place in the western United States called **Yellowstone National Park**. They saw boiling rivers, hot pools that look like they have no end, and geysers that blast water high into the air.

The first explorer believed to have seen this extreme place was a man named John Colter. But, American Indians had already known about the area for hundreds of years. They used the hot springs in Yellowstone for healing and other rites. They also used the hard, black stone found there to make arrowheads and tools. This rock is called *obsidian*. Both the stone and the hot springs are there because of a volcano.

The last time the Yellowstone volcano erupted, it left behind a huge hole, or *crater*. This crater covers almost half of the park. Earth's crust is much thinner in Yellowstone than in other places. That is why there are more than 10,000 hot water features that the volcano created in the park, including hot springs and geysers.

There are more geysers in Yellowstone National Park than anywhere else on Earth. The world's largest geyser, named Steamboat, is also there. When it erupts, Steamboat shoots more than 300 feet of water into the air. It is a very unpredictable geyser. Sometimes, big eruptions occur within weeks. Other times, it can be many years between eruptions.

Old Faithful is the most famous geyser in the park. This geyser shoots water close to 180 feet straight into the air. It was named Old Faithful because it erupts on a very regular schedule. On average, it erupts every 90 minutes. There are many other geysers in the park, too. Some of their names are Plume, Beehive, Castle, and Daisy.

There are also many hot springs and pools in the park. One of the most famous pools is called Morning Glory. It was once a clear, blue pool, shaped like a flower. But, visitors to the park have harmed it. They threw coins and rocks into the pool. This plugged the vent that kept the pool warm. Now, the pool is cooling and growing orange and yellow algae. The beautiful blue colors are turning green. That is one way that people have changed things in Yellowstone National Park.

Conversions

300 feet = 91.44 meters
180 feet = 54.86 meters

Next Page

Extremely Active

Answer the following questions based on what you read on page 55. Then, finish reading the story on the next page.

1. The first part of the story is MOSTLY about—

   a. the beauties of Yellowstone.
   b. the hot springs, geysers, and pools in Yellowstone.
   c. the features of Yellowstone that have been created by the volcano.
   d. b. and c.

2. What is *obsidian*?

   a. a hard, black rock
   b. a type of bird
   c. a volcanic hot spring
   d. none of the above

3. Who was John Colter?

   a. He was the first American Indian to see Yellowstone.
   b. He was probably the first explorer to see Yellowstone.
   c. He was the person who made Yellowstone a national park.
   d. He was the chief of a tribe of Lakota Sioux.

4. What did the Morning Glory pool look like before people harmed it?

   a. It had yellow sides and was very deep.
   b. It held clear blue water.
   c. It was shaped like a flower.
   d. b. and c.

5. Why was Old Faithful given its name?

   a. Its water stays clear and clean.
   b. It erupts at noon every day.
   c. It erupts at times that are easy to predict.
   d. It is the only geyser in the park.

6. Read the following sentence from the story and answer the question.

   They used the hot springs in Yellowstone for healing and other rites.

   Which word could replace *rites* in this sentence?

   a. parties
   b. ceremonies
   c. illnesses
   d. diseases

7. What do you think the author will write about next? Write your answer in a complete sentence.

   _____

   _____

   _____

   _____

   _____

Next Page

**Finish reading "Extremely Active" below.
Then, answer the questions on page 58.**

Visitors to the park have also changed other things about this wild place. People in the park have tamed some of the animals. Prairie dogs that were once wild now wait for people to feed them. Sometimes, they stand in lines along the paths, begging for treats!

Other animals in the park are not tame, even if people think that they are. This has led to some problems. Some people think that the bears of Yellowstone are tame. They are not. They can be a danger to people who get too close to them. It can be especially dangerous to get too close to a mother bear and her cubs. People are a danger to the bears, too. One popular grizzly bear, named Obsidian by the rangers, was hit by a car in 2003. The park rangers tried to help her. But sadly, she was hurt too badly to save.

Other wildlife in the park include moose, eagles, buffalo, wolves, and elk. It is possible for park visitors to see all of these animals as they hike on the trails and drive along the park's roads. The animals can also be seen swimming, eating, and drinking water at the many streams and lakes.

What other sights are there in this strange and beautiful place? There are mountains, valleys, a canyon, and a huge lake. Yellowstone Lake is the largest mountain lake in the United States. The Grand Canyon of Yellowstone is a large, rocky canyon with a 308-foot waterfall on one end. There are broad valleys throughout the park where visitors can see herds of elk, packs of wolves, and sometimes, a family of moose.

But, the hot springs, geysers, and other creations of the volcano make Yellowstone truly unique. Maybe that is why it was chosen in 1872 to be the first national park in the United States. Even though people have harmed parts of the park, Yellowstone is still a grand and exciting place. It offers many natural wonders that cannot be seen anywhere else in the world.

Conversion
308 feet = 93.88 meters

Next Page

Extremely Active

Answer the questions below.

8. Which of the following is NOT mentioned in the story?

   a. Yellowstone's animals
   b. Yellowstone's plants
   c. Yellowstone's water features
   d. Yellowstone's volcano

9. In what way have visitors harmed Yellowstone National Park?

   a. Visitors have clogged pools and springs with coins and rocks.
   b. Visitors have fed the animals and caused some of them to become tame.
   c. Visitors have accidentally hurt animals with their cars.
   d. all of the above

10. Read the following sentence from the story and answer the question.

    But, the hot springs, geysers, and other creations of the volcano make Yellowstone truly unique.

    What does *unique* mean as it is used in this sentence?

    a. unlike any other
    b. usual
    c. unsettling
    d. strange

11. Why is it unsafe to tame the animals in the park?

    a. They learn to trust people too much and can get hit by cars.
    b. They depend on people for their food instead of finding it for themselves.
    c. Even a tamed animal might bite a person if it is scared.
    d. all of the above

12. Which of the following is the name of a geyser in Yellowstone?

    a. Rose
    b. Pansy
    c. Daisy
    d. Clover

13. If you were a park ranger at Yellowstone, would you rather work with the animals or at the water features? Why? Write your answer in complete sentences.

    _____

    _____

    _____

    _____

    _____

Earth's Most Extreme

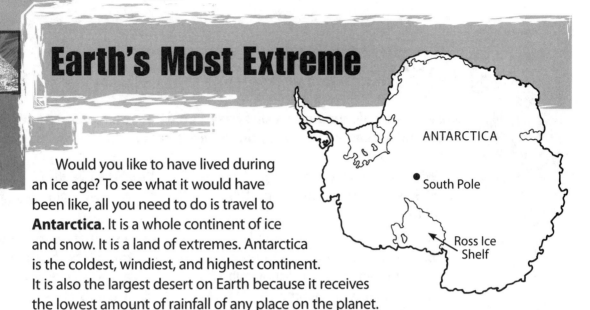

ANTARCTICA

● South Pole

Ross Ice Shelf

Would you like to have lived during an ice age? To see what it would have been like, all you need to do is travel to **Antarctica**. It is a whole continent of ice and snow. It is a land of extremes. Antarctica is the coldest, windiest, and highest continent. It is also the largest desert on Earth because it receives the lowest amount of rainfall of any place on the planet. And, even though it is the highest continent, it also has the lowest place on Earth that is not underwater. The Bentley Subglacial Trench is at least 8,375 feet below sea level. Scientists are not sure how deep the trench is because it is filled with ice.

During winter, Antarctica grows twice as large as it is in the summer. Shelves of ice form in the sea around its coast. In fact, 90 percent of Earth's ice is found in Antarctica. A range of mountains cuts this icy place into two parts. Even parts of the mountains are buried in ice! And, the ice in Antarctica is always moving. Rivers of ice flow from higher ground. They build ice shelves around the lower ground and even out over the seawater. Some of these shelves are huge and stay in place, like the Ross Ice Shelf. It is the size of the state of Texas! Other shelves are smaller and break apart. When a shelf breaks apart, the pieces can form icebergs that float around the coastal waters of Antarctica like white, moving islands.

The temperatures in Antarctica are extreme, too. In winter, it is often as cold as -40°F. Sometimes, the temperature drops below -100°F. But, in the summer, the temperature warms to around 15°F in some parts of the continent. Then, it is possible to see small patches of bare ground. There are very few plants that can live in the extreme temperatures of this place. No crops can grow there. There are no trees in this world of ice and snow. But, Antarctica does have 350 different types of mosses, algae, and lichens. *Lichens* form when fungus grows together with algae on rocks or tree trunks. There are also two types of small plants that grow tiny flowers.

Conversions

8,375 feet = 2,552.7 meters
-40°F = -40°C
-100°F = -73.33°C
15°F = 9.44°C

The continent is home to a small variety of animals, including seals and penguins. Whales, ice fish, and squid live in the water. And, a few types of birds nest on the continent. But, the rarest animal in this world of ice is the human being.

Next Page →

Earth's Most Extreme

Answer the following questions based on what you read on page 59. Then, finish reading the story on the next page.

1. Which of the following is the BEST summary of the first part of the story?

   a. Antarctica is a very cold place.
   b. Antarctica is a very extreme continent of ice and snow with few plants and animals.
   c. Antarctica is the most extreme place on Earth.
   d. Antarctica is cold, icy, and lonely.

2. Which of the following is true?

   a. Crops can be grown in Antarctica.
   b. Penguins live in Antarctica.
   c. Two types of trees grow in Antarctica.
   d. No plants grow in Antarctica.

3.–7. Write T for true or F for false.

3. _____ Antarctica is not a continent.

4. _____ In the summer in Antarctica, the temperature is usually around -15°F.

5. _____ Polar bears live in Antarctica.

6. _____ Whales live in the water around Antarctica.

7. _____ Seals cannot live in Antarctica because it is too cold there.

8. What is an *ice shelf*?

   a. ice that builds from flowing ice rivers
   b. a shelf of ice that grows over the ground or the open sea
   c. a shelf of ice carved by people
   d. a. and b.

9. The Ross Ice Shelf is—

   a. the size of Texas.
   b. an ice shelf that does not move.
   c. an ice shelf that was formed by ice flowing from higher to lower ground.
   d. all of the above

10. What do you think the author will write about next? Write your answer in a complete sentence.

   _____

   _____

   _____

   _____

   _____

Conversion
-15°F = -26.11°C

Next Page

Finish reading "Earth's Most Extreme" below.
Then, answer the questions on page 62.

There are few humans in this cold and extreme place, and none of them are natives. People first came to Antarctica to explore and map the continent. There was also a race to be the first person to reach the South Pole. A team of Norwegians reached the pole first in 1911. Scientists who have studied the South Pole have discovered an interesting fact about the weather there. Even though Antarctica has some of the harshest weather on Earth, the weather at the South Pole is the clearest and calmest on the planet.

Today in Antarctica, there are many *stations*, or bases, where scientists live and work. There are more than 35 stations that are open year-round and at least 15 stations that are open only during the summer. McMurdo, one of the largest stations, can house up to 1,200 people. It is run by the United States. Bellinghausen, one of the smaller stations, is run by Russia. It can house 50 people. Scientists come to the continent to study weather and climate changes, sea life, the glaciers, and the stars, among other things. Most people stay for six months or one year at a time.

What is it like to live in the most extreme place on Earth? It is not like living anywhere else. People do not go outside alone. They always go with at least one other person. They watch each other to make sure they do not freeze! The days in Antarctica sometimes seem like they are all the same. That is because the sun rises only once each year and then sets six months later. That means that there are six months of daylight followed by six months of darkness every year.

But, life in the stations can be quite comfortable. The larger stations have big labs for scientists. One of the stations even has an aquarium. People eat in cafeterias, and some stations have coffee shops. Scientists sleep in dorm rooms. In the summer, people often have to share rooms. In the winter, when there are smaller crews, everyone has a private room. Outside, in the great world of ice, the only colors are blue and white. It is very quiet. Scientists who work there say that Antarctica can seem bleak, but it is also very beautiful.

Next Page

Earth's Most Extreme

Answer the questions below.

11. Read the following sentence from the story and answer the question.

    Scientists who work there say that Antarctica can seem bleak, but it is also very beautiful.

    What is a synonym for *bleak*?

    a. huge
    b. gentle
    c. dreary
    d. bright

12. The story mentions all of the following EXCEPT—

    a. why scientists go to Antarctica.
    b. how many scientists go to Antarctica.
    c. where scientists live in Antarctica.
    d. what scientists study in Antarctica.

13. Which of the following is the name of a station in Antarctica?

    a. Bellingham
    b. Bellinghouse
    c. Bellinghausen
    d. Bellinghauser

14. Living in a station in Antarctica would probably be MOST like—

    a. living in a luxury hotel.
    b. living at a boarding school or college.
    c. living on a tropical island.
    d. living in a large town or city.

15. According to the story, what would life be like if you worked in Antarctica?

    a. You would be doing experiments and scientific work.
    b. There would be days with no sunlight at all.
    c. You would be living in a world with very little color.
    d. all of the above

16. What is one extreme that is NOT found in Antarctica?

    a. extreme rainfall
    b. extreme cold
    c. extreme ice
    d. extreme wind

17. If you went to live at a station in Antarctica, what one thing would you be sure to bring with you? Why? Write your answer in complete sentences.

    _____

    _____

    _____

    _____

    _____

    _____

STOP

Answer Key

Page 6
1. c. 2. b. 3. d.
4. 450, rain, summer
5. c.
6. wet, windy
7. replant

Page 8
1. c. 2. d.
3. Andes
4. Rain Forest
5. no
6. b. 7. b.
8. Answers will vary.

Page 10
1. d.
2. Native Australians named
   the rock Uluru.
3. c. 4. T 5. F 6. F
7. F 8. T 9. d.
10. gigantic, giant, large

Page 12
1. d. 2. c. 3. a.
4. five
5. Colorado
6. six million
7. 1 mile
8. a.
9. The Grand Canyon has five
   different life zones because
   it is so large and deep. The
   different elevations have
   different climates and
   different amounts of water.

Page 14
1. When corals die, their hard
   skeletons remain. Rocks and
   sand wash between the
   skeletons. New coral grows on
   top of the old skeletons, and
   the layers of a coral reef build
   over time.
2. c. 3. F 4. F
5. T 6. T 7. T
8. d. 9. b. 10. c.

Page 16
1. a. 2. d. 3. b.
4. d. 5. c.
6. Answers will vary.

Page 18
1. c. 2. c. 3. a.
4. d. 5. b. 6. c.
7. Answers will vary.

Page 20
1. c. 2. e. 3. a. 4. b.
5. d. 6. b. 7. c.
8. a big pile of dinosaur bones
9. melting ice at the end of the
   last ice age
10. 38
11. b.
12. Answers will vary.

Page 22
1. Tides
2. Wolfville
3. a few
4. 45
5. d. 6. b. 7. a.
8. Answers will vary.

Page 24
1. d. 2. a. 3. c.
4. b. 5. a.
6. Only 50 miles of land
   separated the two
   oceans there.

Page 26
1. b. 2. a. 3. b.
4. d. 5. F 6. T
7. T 8. F 9. a.

Page 28
1. c. 2. b. 3. c. 4. d.
5. Hiram Bingham
6. 1400s
7. Andes
8. cut (or cut to fit)
9. staircases

Page 30
1. b. 2. b.
3. Answers will vary but may
   include:
   a. when they were built
   b. how they were built
   c. how long it took to
      build them
4. c. 5. c.
6. Answers will vary.

Page 31
the people who live
in Verkhoyansk

Page 32
1. d. 2. d.
3. The temperature can drop to
   -90°F in Verkhoyansk.
4. difficult, frigid, dark

Page 33
5. b.   6. b.   7. a.
8. c.   9. c.
10. Answers will vary.

Page 34
how scientists know that there was once more water in the Sahara

Page 35
1. b.   2. c.   3. c.

Page 36
4. F   5. F   6. T   7. T
8. b.   9. d.   10. b.
11. Answers will vary.

Page 37
the solution to the mystery of the huge statues and the strange, bare island

Page 38
1. Jacob Roggevenn
2. statues
3. Pacific
4. trees
5. c.   6. d.

Page 39
7. c.   8. a.   9. b.   10. c.
11. Answers will vary.

Page 40
what happened in the 1860s to let the world know about the city of Angkor

Page 41
1. Answers will vary but may include:
   a. rich (or golden)
   b. beautiful
   c. like something from a dream
2. d.   3. d.

Page 42
4. 70, carvings
5. c.   6. b.   7. c.   8. d.
9. Answers will vary.

Page 43
what scientists have learned about the city of Petra

Page 44
1. d.   2. c.   3. c.
4. Answers will vary but may include: extraordinary, hidden, beautiful, rich, protected

Page 45
5. b.   6. a.   7. b.
8. b.   9. c.
10. Answers will vary.

Page 46
what the survivors found when they returned to Pompeii

Page 47
1. F   2. F   3. T   4. T
5. F   6. c.   7. a.

Page 48
8. d.   9. b.   10. b.
11. d.   12. c.
13. Pompeii was destroyed by the volcano because it was buried, and many people died. The city was "saved" by the volcano because it was preserved forever, which allowed modern scientists to study it and learn about its people.

Page 49
people who have tried to climb Mount Everest

Page 50
1. avalanche   2. clouds
3. Glaciers   4. highest
5. Answers will vary but may include: dangerous, tall, high, unpredictable, cold

Page 51
6. d.   7. b.   8. c.
9. a.   10. d.
11. Answers will vary.

Page 52
the fish and animals of the Amazon River

Page 53
1. c.   2. a.   3. d.

Page 54
4. c.   5. a.   6. c.   7. b.
8. Answers will vary.

Page 56
1. d.   2. a.   3. b.
4. d.   5. c.   6. b.
7. The author will describe other things that visitors have changed in the park.

Page 58
8. b.   9. d.   10. a.
11. d.   12. c.
13. Answers will vary.

Page 60
1. b.   2. b.   3. F
4. F   5. F   6. T
7. F   8. d.   9. d.
10. The author will write about humans in Antarctica.

Page 62
11. c.   12. b.   13. c.
14. b.   15. d.   16. a.
17. Answers will vary.